20 Answers

≈

Abortion

Trent Horn

Catholic
Answers
Press

20 Answers Abortion

Trent Horn

© 2014 Catholic Answers

Published by Catholic Answers, Inc.

2020 Gillespie Way

El Cajon, California 92020

1-888-291-8000 orders

619-387-0042 fax

catholic.com

Printed in the United States of America

ISBN 978-1-938983-81-8 paperback

ISBN 978-1-938983-82-5 Kindle

ISBN 978-1-938983-83-2 ePub

Introduction

In 2012 the Gallup polling service released a study indicating that for the first time a majority of Americans identified themselves as being pro-life.[1] This should have been a cause for celebration among pro-life advocates, but 2012 also revealed that America is not ready to outlaw abortion. Not only did America re-elect a president who was firmly committed to keeping abortion legal, but ballot initiatives that could have severely restricted or outlawed abortion at the state level also failed to pass. In fact, since 1973 no state has ever successfully voted to outlaw a majority of abortions that occur.

What explains the actions of people who say they are pro-life but refuse to take steps to make abortion illegal? One explanation is that the term *pro-life* refers to those who merely dislike abortion but do not think it is a serious moral wrong. In fact, one study found that 35 percent of self-described pro-lifers did not want *Roe v. Wade* (the Supreme Court Case that keeps abortion legal) overturned.[2] These people may not choose abortion for themselves, but they do not want to make abortion illegal in general.

While pro-life advocates have done an excellent job of showing that the unborn are alive and human (such as through new ultrasound technology), the opposition has retreated behind new arguments that must be answered. Some of these "pro-lifers" who support legal abortion say that they can't "impose their morality" on anyone else. They may think that other issues—such as ending sex trafficking or poverty—are more important than abortion. Or they may think that even if the unborn are human beings, a woman has a right not to let her child use her body without her consent.

Pro-life advocates must refocus their efforts to communicate an attractive and powerful defense of unborn children. Along with answering these new arguments for legal abortion, pro-life advocates can be successful by simply communicating simple statements of fact. For example, a 2013 NBC/*Wall Street Journal* poll found that while 70 percent of Americans did not want *Roe v. Wade* overturned, 41 percent in the same poll said they did not know enough about *Roe v. Wade* to say if they disapproved of it.[3] A 2012 Pew Research poll found that 57 percent of adults under the age of thirty did not even know what *Roe v. Wade* had decided.[4] For these people, the idea of *anything* being overturned was enough to draw their opposition.

The goal of this booklet is to show that the questions presented by critics of the pro-life position can be answered in a gracious way with scientific facts and sound, logical reasoning. Those people who believe in human equality, the dignity of the human person, and the duty to care for the least among us should seriously consider accepting the pro-life position and stand up for the right to life of unborn children.

1. What is abortion?

Defining abortion can be difficult, because both sides of the issue tend to use language that favors their opinion of the procedure. For example, people who believe abortion should be legal (who call themselves "pro-choice") often define abortion as the termination of a pregnancy or the emptying of the contents of the uterus. In contrast, people who believe abortion should be illegal (who call themselves "pro-life") often define abortion as the killing of a baby or the killing of an unborn human being.

So is abortion a morally innocuous emptying of the uterus, or is it child-killing? If pro-choice people are right and an abortion is harmless surgery, then restrictions on abortion would hurt women and make them second-class citizens. If pro-life people are right and abortion kills a valuable human being, then keeping abortion legal would be the continuation of a tremendous evil that has taken tens of millions of innocent lives. So which side is right, and how should we respond?

According to the *Oxford English Dictionary*, abortion is "the expulsion or removal from the womb of a developing embryo or fetus in the period before it is capable of independent survival." This distinguishes abortion from childbirth, when an unborn child is removed from the womb when he can survive and there is no intention of killing him.

Abortions are either spontaneous (usually referred to as *miscarriages*) or intentional (called *induced abortions*). The majority of induced abortions are elective, meaning they are done for social and non-health-related reasons. The most common reasons women give for having an abortion are: "Having a baby would dramatically change my life" (74 percent), "I can't afford a baby right now" (73 percent), and "I don't want to be a single mother or am having relationship problems" (48 percent).[5]

About 90 percent of the 1.06 million abortions performed in the United States each year occur in the first trimester of pregnancy. During this stage of pregnancy the abortion provider administers medication that causes something similar to a miscarriage, or he uses a tube connected to a vacuum to suck out the unborn human being from the uterus. If the latter procedure is used, the abortion provider will usually collect the child's body parts in a jar and examine them to make sure none were left inside the mother.

In the later stages of pregnancy, when the unborn human is too big to fit through the vacuum tube, the abortion provider uses a procedure called dilation and evacuation (or D&E). This brutal procedure is described in the Supreme Court case *Gonzales v. Carhart* (2007):

> The doctor, often guided by ultrasound, inserts grasping forceps through the woman's cervix and

into the uterus to grab the fetus. The doctor grips a fetal part with the forceps and pulls it back through the cervix and vagina, continuing to pull even after meeting resistance from the cervix. The friction causes the fetus to tear apart. For example, a leg might be ripped off the fetus as it is pulled through the cervix and out of the woman. The process of evacuating the fetus piece by piece continues until it has been completely removed.[6]

Another reason abortion is such an emotional issue is that millions of women are post-abortive. It is estimated that one in every three women by age 45 will have had at least one abortion.[7] The grisly reality of abortion can cause these women and their partners to have deep feelings of regret and guilt. When talking about the reality of abortion, it is important not to lose sight of these men and women and to let them know that they can find healing and hope. In his encyclical *The Gospel of Life*, Pope John Paul II wrote in a special message to post-abortive women:

The Church is aware of the many factors which may have influenced your decision, and she does not doubt that in many cases it was a painful and even shattering decision. . . . The Father of mercies is ready to give you his forgiveness and his peace in the Sacrament of Reconciliation. To the same

Father and his mercy you can with sure hope entrust your child.[8]

2. What is the legal status of abortion in the United States?

Throughout U.S. history abortion was illegal except in rare cases when the woman's life was in danger or if the pregnancy resulted from rape or incest. That changed when Norma McCorvey, under the pseudonym Jane Roe, sued the state of Texas for her alleged right to have an abortion. On January 22, 1973, the Supreme Court handed down its *Roe v. Wade* decision, ruling 7 to 2 in favor of Roe.

Justice Harry Blackmun wrote the Court's majority opinion. In it he claimed that the U.S. Constitution contains an implicit "right to privacy," and since abortion is a private decision between a woman and her doctor, it follows that states cannot outlaw abortion. Furthermore, Blackmun claimed that scientists, doctors, and other experts do not agree on whether or not an unborn child is a human being, and so the Court could not settle the matter (though it would seem the Supreme Court implicitly ruled unborn children are *not* human beings by making it legal to kill them).[9]

Roe v. Wade divided pregnancy into three twelve-week "trimesters." The Court ruled that in the first two trimesters, or first twenty-four weeks of pregnancy, states could not outlaw abortion. In the second trimester, states could regulate the procedure so that it is safe for the mother. In the third trimester of pregnancy, *Roe v. Wade* allowed (but did not require) states to ban abortion. If states banned abortion in the third trimester, they had to allow an exception for abortions deemed necessary to protect a woman's health.

While fewer than 1 percent of abortions occur in the late second and third trimesters of pregnancy, this translates to about 10,000 annual abortions at these stages of fetal development. To put that into perspective, according to the FBI, 8,500 people are murdered by firearms in the U.S. every year.[10] That means that in the United States, more human beings are killed every year by late-term abortion than are killed by guns.

One major problem with the third-trimester health exception is that *Roe*'s companion case, *Doe v. Bolton*, ruled that "health" can include any factor that is "physical, emotional, psychological, familial, [or related to] the woman's age."[11] Abortion provider Warren Hern has even argued that a child being unwanted by his mother can be considered a "health risk" to the pregnancy: "It appears that 'unwantedness' may be regarded as a major complication of pregnancy with surgical intervention in the form of abortion as the indicated treatment."[12] The Court's definition of health thus made it almost impossible to ban any abortions. Today a woman can obtain an abortion through all nine months of pregnancy for virtually any reason.

This fact has motivated millions of people to oppose abortion and campaign to make it illegal again—including Norma McCorvey, who converted to the pro-life position and now travels the country educating others about the awful consequences of *Roe v. Wade*.[13]

3. What's wrong with being pro-choice? No one is forcing pro-life people to have abortions. Why can't other people have the right to choose whether or not they want to be parents and use abortion if it is right for them?

Both pro-choice and pro-life people agree that women should be allowed to choose many things in life. They should be allowed to choose their religion, their careers, their husbands, and whether or not they want to be parents. There is nothing wrong with choice itself, so long as what is being chosen is a moral good.

For example, a woman who chooses not to be a parent by choosing not to marry and leading a single life devoted to serving God and her community chooses something that is very good. Likewise, a married couple who choose, for good reasons, to avoid conception through natural and moral means, also choose something that is good.

However, when a couple choose not to be parents by smothering their born child and throwing his body into a dumpster, they choose a bad thing. In fact, they choose something that is so bad that it should be illegal. When a pro-choice advocate says, "Women should have the right to choose," we must always ask the follow-up question, "The right to choose what?"

The central issue related to abortion is not "choice," because, as we've seen, there are many good things people should be allowed to choose. The central issue also isn't the freedom to have or not have children, because pro-life advocates agree men and women should not be forced to conceive a child against their will.

Instead, the central issue in the abortion debate is "What are the unborn?" When a pro-choice advocate says women should be able to choose not to be mothers, he is assuming that the act of abortion is contraceptive and only *prevents* a child from coming into existence. Pro-life advocates agree that women should be able to choose whether or not they want to be mothers, but if a woman is pregnant, it is simply the case that she is *already* a mother. She is a mother because she has a tiny human being growing inside of her.

Having an abortion doesn't prevent a child from coming into existence; it violently takes a child out of existence. Just as we wouldn't tolerate parents' killing their two-year-old because they "did not want to be parents" (in the biological as well as the legal sense of the word), we should not tolerate parents' killing their unborn child for the same reason.

If the unborn are human, then the position of

"pro-choice" is not a compromise position that each side can embrace. Saying that pro-life advocates should not work to outlaw abortion because they aren't forced to have abortions ("Don't like abortion? Then don't have one!") is like saying feminists should not outlaw spousal abuse because they aren't forced to abuse their own spouses ("Don't like beating your spouse? Don't beat him!").

Tolerance is acceptable when it is applied to nuisances, such as a noisy child. However, injustice—such as forcing a child to work in a coal mine—must never be tolerated. Good people must work hard to eradicate injustice, even when the injustice doesn't personally affect them. That is because all people have intrinsic dignity and worth, and as human beings we have a responsibility to care for our neighbor, regardless of who they are.

4. Is it possible to know when life begins, or is this just a religious belief that can't be answered?

The question "When does life begin?" actually contains two distinct questions. First, there is the question "When does a biological human being, or an organism of the species *Homo sapiens*, come into existence?" This is a scientific question that is not seriously disputed among academics on both sides of the abortion debate.

The second question is "When does a human being with rights, or a *person*, come into existence?" This is a philosophical or religious question, because people associate different meanings with the term *person*. In order to answer the question of whether or not an unborn child is a person, we must first answer the question of whether or not an unborn child is a biological human being, i.e., a younger member of our species. After all, you can't have human rights unless you are a biological human being.

So how can we know the unborn are human beings in the biological sense of the word?

We can start by observing that the unborn are alive. We know this because the unborn child's body takes in nutrients that are converted into energy that allows the child to grow and develop. In fact, the unborn child's heart begins to beat about three weeks after he is conceived.[14] Of course, being alive is not what makes something human, because trees and bacteria are alive. Instead, the unborn are human because they possess human DNA and are the result of the union of two members of the human species.

Some critics say that the unborn are not human but are merely fetuses, but this is a misunderstanding of what the word *fetus* means. *Fetus* is a Latin word that means "young one." It designates a particular stage of development in the life of a human being. In fact, from conception until the seventh week of life the unborn child is called an *embryo*; then from eight weeks until birth he is called a *fetus*; then after birth he is called an *infant* and then a *toddler* and so on. Saying an unborn child is not human because he is a "fetus" makes as much sense as saying a fifteen-year-old is not human because he is a "teenager."

Finally, the unborn are whole human organisms and are not a part of someone else's body. It is true that sperm, egg, and other body cells such as skin cells are alive and possess human DNA. However, even if these things are given time, nutrition, and a proper environment, they can never develop into an adult human being. In contrast, you and I are organisms, because if we are given time, nutrition, and a proper environment (e.g., not on the moon or at the bottom of the ocean), we will continue to develop more and more into mature members of the human species.

Likewise, an unborn child, when given time, nutrition, and a proper environment (e.g., not outside the uterus), will develop into a mature human being if he does not die prematurely. Embryologist E.L. Potter agrees and says that "every time a sperm cell and ovum unite, a new being is created which is alive and will continue to live unless its death is brought about by some specific condition."[15]

The fact that an unborn child is a human organism is not seriously disputed among scientists and philosophers. The standard medical text *Human Embryology and Teratology* states, "Although human life is a continuous process, fertilization [also called conception] is a critical landmark because, under ordinary circumstances, a new, genetically distinct human organism is thereby formed."[16] Pro-choice philosopher David Boonin writes in his book *A Defense of Abortion*, "[T]he most straightforward relation between you and me on the one hand and every human fetus on the other is this: All are living members of the same species, *homo sapiens*. A human fetus after all is simply a human being at a very early stage in his or her development."[17]

5. Even if a fetus is biologically human, how do we know a fetus is "fully" human, or a person with rights? After all, a fetus can't think or feel, and it can't survive on its own. Can we really say something like that is a person?

In order to answer the question "Is the fetus a person?" we must first answer an even more important set of questions: "What is a person? Are there human beings who are not persons?" Every time in history when certain human beings were disqualified from being considered persons (African-Americans, women, Jews, the mentally handicapped, etc.), the reason justifying their disqualification turned out to be bogus.

Since human beings differ in size, intelligence, skin color, gender, physical ability, and a host of other attributes, we must ground human equality in the one thing that truly makes all of us equal: our human nature. Specifically, what makes humans "persons" is that they belong to a rational kind of being: in this case, the human species. This definition of person-hood applies to humans who are members of our kind who are not yet rational (such as infants) as well as humans who have lost their ability to be rational (such as the disabled). There are also persons who are not human because they belong to another rational kind, such as angels. However, the important point is that all human beings belong to our species, and therefore all humans are persons.

What about other definitions of personhood that pro-choice advocates embrace that do not rest on our common humanity? Should we adopt these definitions that might exclude the unborn? We should if there is a compelling reason to think any of these definitions of person-hood are correct. But there are in fact many reasons to think these alternate definitions of personhood are false.

For example, some pro-choice advocates say that a person is someone who can think, or feel pain. While it's true that unborn children do not become aware of the outside world or feel pain until late in pregnancy, this does not mean they are not persons. After all, people in comas and even those who are asleep are not aware of the outside world, and no one would say they are not persons.[18]

In addition, animals such as rats can feel pain and

possess rudimentary thinking abilities, but this does not make them persons. A pro-choice advocate could respond by saying that anyone who can think beyond the level of an animal is a person, but this would exclude infants as well as unborn children, because at neither stage can a human outperform an animal when it comes to rational thought.

Other pro-choice advocates say that a person is anyone who can survive outside of the womb. Since an unborn child is totally dependent on his mother's body before a point called *viability* (which is usually twenty-four weeks after conception), he cannot survive being removed from the uterus. But how does this show he is not a person? After all, animals can survive outside of the womb, but that doesn't make them persons. Furthermore, if an infant is left alone after birth, he is not "viable" and will die without assistance, but that doesn't mean he is not a person. This shows that viability is irrelevant to whether or not someone is a person.

A critic could argue that instead of there being a moment when a fetus becomes a person, a fetus *gradually* becomes a person. Under this view, smaller or less developed embryos are less human, but as they grow into fetuses, they gradually become more and more human until they are fully human at birth. However, there is no logical reason for the gradualist to maintain that the fetus gradually becomes a person until it is *born*, when it suddenly becomes a complete person. Why not say fetuses gradually become persons until they become fully human at the age of two or even twenty-two?

While it's true that humans gradually gain other rights after birth, such as the right to drive or to vote, most critics agree that humans don't gradually gain *basic* rights after birth. For example, we don't say five-year-olds are halfway to having the right not to be tortured. If it's absurd to believe that born humans gradually acquire basic rights, such as the right to life, then wouldn't it be absurd to say that *unborn* humans gradually acquire those same basic rights?

The most sensible view of personhood is that all humans are equal in virtue of the one thing that makes us all equal: our human nature. The pro-life position is simply that all humans, regardless of race, gender, age, or level of development, should be treated equally and not be killed simply because they are unwanted.

6. Even if the fetus is a person, shouldn't women still have the right to control their own bodies?

Pro-life advocates certainly agree that both men and women should be allowed to control their own bodies and not have them invaded by the government or anyone else. However, abortion is not just one person making modifications to her own body (such as getting a tattoo or plastic surgery) but is one person using her body to hurt another person who lives inside of that body. An unborn child is not like an appendix or another body part we can remove without serious moral consequences. We've already seen that the unborn child is a distinct human organism with its own set of DNA.

But even if the unborn are separate human beings who are distinct from their mothers, should that matter if women have the right to do whatever they want with their own bodies? The problem with this argument for abortion is that it is based on a controversial premise—the premise that we have the right to do *anything* we want with our bodies. After all, everyone agrees we should not be allowed to pummel another person to death with our fists. Pro-choice critics might respond that the right to control our bodies means we have a right to control only things *inside* our bodies, which would include the right to remove an unborn child.

But if such a right really existed, then the state would have no justification for banning other bodily acts, such as the use of narcotic drugs or public displays of nudity. In *Roe v. Wade* the Supreme Court rejected this argument for legal abortion. The Court said, "[I]t is not clear to us that the claim asserted by some *amici* that one has an unlimited right to do with one's body as one pleases bears a close relationship to the right of privacy previously articulated in the Court's decisions. The Court has refused to recognize an unlimited right of this kind in the past."[19]

Virtually no other rights that society recognizes are unlimited like the so-called right to bodily autonomy. Freedom of speech does not allow someone to falsely shout, "Fire!" in a crowded building. Freedom of religion does not allow someone to marry multiple people. The right to bear arms does not allow someone to own a nuclear missile.

If pregnant women had a right to do anything with their bodies, it would lead to all kinds of absurd situations. It would mean that doctors could not deny pregnant women drugs like thalidomide, which, while effective at reducing nausea in pregnancy, also can cause babies to be born without arms or legs. Even more absurd, there would be nothing immoral in taking a healthy prematurely born infant out of a hospital incubator, reinserting him in his mother's womb, and then killing him.

Although people don't have the right to do whatever they want with their bodies, all people do have a right to control their bodies to a certain extent, and this implies that they have a right to their bodily integrity even when they are not conscious. For example, an unconscious woman in a hospital has the right not to be molested by a male nurse, even though she would not be aware of being violated. We see in this case that the right to control one's body also includes the right not to have one's body violated. But if that is true, and the unborn are human beings who have the same rights as you and I, then unborn children would also have a right to "control their own bodies." Logically, it would follow that they have a right not to have their bodies torn apart by abortion, and therefore abortion should be illegal.

7. Perhaps women can't do whatever they want with their own bodies, but why should they be forced to keep their fetuses alive against their will? We would never force a parent to donate his kidney in order to save his own child's life, so why should we force pregnant women to donate their bodies to keep their fetuses alive?

Some pro-choice advocates say that we all have the right to refuse to donate our bodies to help other people, even if that refusal would cause someone else to die. Therefore, pregnant women have the right to refuse to "donate" the use of their bodies to their unborn children.

Pro-life advocates agree that things like mandatory organ donations would be a gross invasion of our right to bodily integrity and privacy. But is pregnancy the same as forcing a parent to donate a kidney in order to keep her born child alive? There are key differences between these two cases that make it immoral for the state to require organ donation but moral for the state to prohibit aborting an unborn child.

First, in the case of organ donation, the parents do not engage in an activity that is designed to cause their child to need the use of their organs. In contrast, when we examine the biological design and function of the genitals and reproductive systems, we reach an unavoidable conclusion: Reproductive organs are for the reproduction of another human being. When men and women engage in sexual relations with those organs, they engage in an activity that is designed to create a helpless human being whom they then have a duty to support.

Secondly, even in cases where a woman is not responsible for the existence of the child she is carrying (such as pregnancies that result from rape), the woman is still the parent of the child and is providing him ordinary care we expect from a parent. A person's kidneys are made to filter his own blood, and we consider it extraordinary, not obligatory, when an adult donates a kidney in order to save someone else's life. But what is the uterus for, and is its function in pregnancy as extraordinary as kidney donation?[20]

Finally, having an abortion is not like refusing to donate a kidney in order to save your child's life. In the kidney case, the child dies from a disease that is unrelated to the actions of his or her parents. When a parent fails to donate an organ to save his child, he does not kill the child; he merely fails to save his child from something that kills him. In contrast, abortion is not the mere "withholding" of an organ that could save a sick child; it is the violent refusal of an organ that is designed to keep a healthy child alive.

Far from being an extraordinary use of an organ, keeping an unborn child alive seems to be the uterus's sole purpose. Rather than being a nice gift a mother grants to her child, providing a safe environment in the womb seems to be a duty mothers have to their children. Pregnancy is certainly difficult and involves dramatic changes to the body, but so do puberty and old age. The fact is that these are ordinary aspects of life, and without the ordinary aspect of pregnancy, no one would exist to read this page. Choosing not to abort one's child is not an act of extraordinary good will; it is the minimal standard of care we expect from parents. This standard applies to both parents, which means men have a duty to provide financial and emotional support for women, and women have a duty to provide a safe environment in the womb for their unborn children.

8. Do you support abortion in the case of rape? I'm not in favor of all abortions, but I do think that if a woman is raped, she should be able to have an abortion, since she never chose to have sex. Plus, having the baby would just add even more trauma on top of the rape.

Rape is a heinous and violent act that no civilized society should ever tolerate. Rape violates a person's bodily integrity and takes away her ability to feel safe even around people she has known for a long time. Even worse, many women are simply not believed when they report being raped. Sometimes they are even blamed for engaging in actions that "caused" them to be raped. This is a completely unacceptable way to treat an innocent victim of violence.

Victims of rape deserve compassion and access to the resources they need to heal as well as the resources to bring their attackers to justice. Paragraph 36 of the *The Ethical and Religious Directives for Catholic Healthcare Services* states:

Compassionate and understanding care should be given to a person who is the victim of sexual assault. Health care providers should cooperate with law enforcement officials and offer the person psychological and spiritual support as well as accurate medical information. A female who has been raped should be able to defend herself against a potential conception from the sexual assault. If, after appropriate testing, there is no evidence that conception has occurred already, she may be treated with medications that would prevent ovulation, sperm capacitation, or fertilization. It is not permissible, however, to initiate or to recommend treatments that have as their purpose or direct effect the removal, destruction, or interference with the implantation of a fertilized ovum.

Women who become pregnant as a result of rape are further victimized because they have been forced to become mothers against their will and now must contemplate choosing abortion, adoption, or parenthood. But notice that it is the *rapist* who is the source of the evil that comes from rape, and he is the one who should be held responsible for his crime.

Just as we should not punish or blame the woman who is a victim of rape but work to provide her with healing, we should not punish or harm the child who is conceived in rape and is also victimized. The child is made a victim by being brought into existence in an act of violence instead of an act of love. Ironically, in our country it is illegal to execute the man who rapes a child, but a child conceived in rape can be killed through abortion.[21]

Here's another way to understand the issue. Imagine that a woman has sexual relations with her husband, and the next day she is raped by a stranger. Several weeks later she discovers she's pregnant but doesn't know if the child was fathered by her husband or the rapist. A DNA test reveals the husband is the child's father. The woman gives birth, and three months later the doctor calls while she is home alone with the baby. He informs her that he made a mistake and that the rapist is actually the baby's father. The woman is devastated and can't stand to have this "thing" grow up who one day might become a rapist himself. Should she be allowed to kill this product of rape in the crib? If not, then shouldn't we forbid killing the product of rape in the womb for the same reason we forbid killing the product of rape in the crib: because both are human beings?[22]

Rape is traumatic because it is an act of violence against an innocent person. Even though critics have good intentions when they suggest that abortion could ease the trauma a victim of rape has faced, how could it be an act of healing to inflict further violence on the innocent child who had nothing to do with the rape itself? Shouldn't we work to protect both the mother and child from harm and punish the person who was truly responsible for the rape?

9. If abortion were made illegal, then women would be forced to get abortions from untrained "back-alley" abortionists. Shouldn't we keep abortion legal so that it's at least safe?

Pro-life advocates are certainly worried about anyone dying from an abortion procedure, whether it's an unborn child or a pregnant woman. We don't want anyone to die from either legal or illegal abortion. Pro-life advocates have no problem with terminating pregnancies so that neither the mother nor the unborn child is killed. This is also called childbirth. It might surprise pro-choice advocates to know that we also believe abortion should be safe—for both the mother and the child. Unfortunately, abortion can never be made safe for the child, because it is designed to end the child's life. It flies in the face of justice to keep a procedure legal in order to make it safer for a bigger person to kill a smaller innocent person.

This objection also tends to exaggerate the scope of illegal abortion prior to *Roe v. Wade*. It's commonly claimed that more than one million illegal abortions occurred each year before *Roe v. Wade*. However, a 1981 study found that prior to legalization, the average number of illegal abortions in the United States was about 98,000, or about 10 percent of what the rate became shortly after *Roe v. Wade*.[23]

Another common claim that circulates around the Internet is that, prior to *Roe v. Wade*, 5,000 to 10,000 women died each year from illegal abortions. However, according to the Centers for Disease Control, only thirty-nine women died from illegal abortion deaths in 1972, and twenty-four women died from legal abortions in the same year.[24] Former Planned Parenthood president Mary Calderone said in 1960:

Abortion is no longer a dangerous procedure. This applies not just to therapeutic abortions as performed in hospitals but also to so-called illegal abortions as done by physicians. In 1957 there were only 260 deaths in the whole country attributed to abortions of any kind. . . . Second, and even more important, the conference estimated that 90 percent of all illegal abortions are presently being done by physicians.[25]

In 2010 the United States had a maternal mortality rate of twenty-one deaths per 100,000 live births. In Ireland and Poland, where abortion is illegal except in rare cases, the maternal mortality rate per 100,000 live births was six deaths and five deaths, respectively.[26] There is no reason to think that a developed country cannot protect the health of both unborn and born human beings.

10. If abortion were made illegal, then what should the punishment be for a woman who chose to have one?

Whether or not women should be punished for having an abortion depends on how we answer another, more fundamental question: "How should people be punished who kill their own children?" The most honest answer is "It depends."

The punishments for crimes vary based on the intent and circumstances surrounding the crimes. Even those found guilty of homicide, or the intentional killing of one human being by another human being, do not receive the same punishments. For example, the wife who kills her husband in order to collect money from his from insurance policy may be punished more severely than the wife who kills her abusive husband, who made her live in a state of constant fear.

Are there any circumstances that should be taken into account when it comes to women who have abortions? For many women, abortion has been legal for their entire lives, and in the United States there are no public education campaigns to discourage women from having an abortion (unlike for other harmful things, such as smoking).

Professional medical organizations endorse abortion, and many women choose abortion when their partners, family, or health care providers suggest it (or when in some cases they are coerced). Finally, most women do not intend to kill their child but instead simply no longer want to be pregnant. They may even think abortion is a form of surgical contraception that keeps a potential person from becoming an "actual baby."

All these factors show that women may not be completely morally responsible for choosing abortion, and so they may not deserve as harsh a punishment as concerned pro-choice advocates think they would receive. This reasoning is not a case of special pleading for the pro-life view, as it is already used to justify lighter sentences for women who kill their born infants.[27]

Infanticide is considered less serious than first-degree murder, because the perpetrators of the former are usually a danger only to their own offspring and are often under extreme emotional stress. Punishments for infanticide can be as light as one to two years' imprisonment or even probation. If abortion were made illegal, "feticide" laws could be enacted that mirror current infanticide laws in language and range of punishments. That way, women who chose abortion, as well as the men who cooperate and the doctors who perform the procedure, would be appropriately punished based on each person's level of moral responsibility.

Finally, isn't it unfair—and logically inconsistent—that in many states, if men or women kill a *wanted* fetus, they are legally punished? Most people do not consider it outrageous that in 2004 Scott Petersen was convicted of two counts of murder for the death of his wife, Laci, and their unborn son, Conner. Why wouldn't we charge Laci with committing a crime if she were to kill her own unborn child?

If we lived in a society that truly believed the unborn were just very small children, then why not treat the killing of the unborn with the equivalent concern we have for the killing of born children? The real question isn't "Should women be punished for having abortions?" but "What punishments should be given for killing a human child?"

11. Would you be against abortion even if the woman's life was in danger or the fetus was going to die anyway?

The pro-life position holds that all human beings have equal value and possess intrinsic rights from the moment they begin to exist (i.e., conception) until the moment they cease to exist (natural death). Just because someone's life is coming to a natural end does not mean he possesses fewer rights than the rest of us.

Let's consider the case of an unborn child who has a severe fetal deformity and will die shortly after birth. One case like this is anencephaly, a condition that occurs when the child fails to develop an upper brain and will die a few hours or days after birth. Is it moral to abort an anencephalic child?

To help us decide if it is moral to abort such a child, imagine the case of a two-year-old who finds his dad's gun and tragically blows off the top of his head. As he lies in the hospital, dying from his injuries (which would mirror the plight of an anencephalic child), we would certainly do everything we could to ease this child's suffering, but we wouldn't outright kill the child. Therefore, we should do everything we can to care for a dying unborn child, but we should not kill him in order to treat his terminal condition.

Furthermore, many abortions done for fetal abnormalities are done on children with nonterminal and even non-debilitating conditions, such as Down syndrome. Recommending abortion in order to resolve a fetal health problem makes as much sense as recommending decapitation in order to resolve a migraine. But what if it is not the child's life that is in danger but the mother's? Should abortion be used in order to save the mother's life?

In cases where a woman's life is in danger, doctors should treat both mother and child as human beings with rights and dignity. Neither mother nor child should be killed simply as a way to save the life of either. What if a woman's life is threatened late in pregnancy, after the fetus is viable? Since it takes longer than a day to stretch the cervix to be wide enough to abort such a large fetus, it makes more sense simply to deliver the child by C-section if one wants to end the pregnancy quickly.[28] Wouldn't it be better to deliver the child whole and give her a chance to live (even if the chance is small) as opposed to delivering him in pieces where he has no chance to live?

When a problem develops early in pregnancy, there is essentially no hope that the child can be saved. In this case, it is permissible for doctors to perform a lifesaving operation on the mother, with the indirect result being the death of the child. The most notable example of this case is an ectopic pregnancy, which occurs when the human embryo implants outside of the uterus in a place such as the fallopian tube. In this case it is morally acceptable to remove the damaged section of the fallopian tube where the child has implanted. This action is moral, because the primary intention is to remove the damaged section of the fallopian tube that is threatening the mother's health.

The child's death is an unintended consequence of this morally neutral action.

It's important to remember that pregnancies in which a mother's life is in danger and the child cannot be delivered are exceedingly rare. According to Thomas Murphy Goodwin, a professor of obstetrics, gynecology, and pediatrics at the University of Southern California, his own medical service routinely sees 15,000 to 16,000 births each year, and, excluding emergencies that occur in the third trimester, he sees no more than one or two cases per year that are life-threatening.[29]

Laws that permitted abortion on demand simply because there are rare, hard cases would be as strange as laws that repealed all speed limits just because there are rare cases in which they need to be ignored to get someone to a hospital. The primary question we must stay focused on is "What are the unborn?" If the unborn are not human, then there are no dilemmas for doctors to face when they treat pregnant women. However, if the unborn are humans, there may be extraordinary situations in which doctors are not sure how ethically to save both mother and child. But these difficult cases do not refute the pro-life position that the unborn are human beings who deserve the right to life.

12. Some women just can't have a baby during difficult times in their lives. What about the fourteen-year-old pregnant girl who will be thrown

out on the street by her parents? Or the mom who can't even feed the children she has now? Surely these women need reproductive options in order to help them with these difficult circumstances.

Living in poverty or feeling too young to care for a child certainly involves difficult circumstances. Both sides of the abortion debate agree that the poor should be provided with practical options so that they can live in dignity and economic security. The real question is not whether these women have "reproductive options" or "the right to choose" but whether women in difficult circumstances should be allowed to abort their children. Let's examine these difficult situations from another perspective.

Imagine that the pregnant fourteen-year-old is living with her boyfriend, and she already has one baby and is pregnant with another. The boyfriend threatens to throw her out unless she "gets rid of" the baby. What if she decided to kill the born baby and keep the unborn child instead? Should that act be legal? Likewise, imagine that the pregnant mom who cannot feed the children she already has kills two of the youngest ones to make room for the new baby who is on the way. Should that act be legal?[30]

Most people would say, "Of course not!" But why not? "Because in those cases a real baby, or a real human being, is killed," the critic may respond.

Then that's the issue. Everyone agrees that even though circumstances like poverty are difficult, those circumstances would not justify killing born children. Likewise, if unborn children are as human as born children, then shouldn't we treat unborn children the same way we treat born children and not kill them because they are unwanted or complicate already difficult circumstances?

This reasoning also applies to other reasons that are given to keep abortion legal that assume the unborn child is not a human being. For example, some people claim that children born to impoverished or young mothers will face a lifetime of abuse and neglect, and abortion is a preferable option. This is debatable, but suppose it were true. Would that justify killing these children before birth? Certainly it seems bizarre that we would try to protect children from possible violence in the future by violently ending their lives before birth, a solution—death—we would never use for a born child.

Another claim pro-choice advocates make in order justify abortion is that the world is overpopulated and the earth cannot sustain an increasing human population. While the reality of overpopulation is disputed, let's simply agree with the critic that the world is overpopulated. Would that justify abortion?

Most people agree we should not round up homeless people, or children in foster-care systems, and kill them in order to ease the strains created by overpopulation. But why is it wrong? It's wrong because human beings have rights and dignity, and it is wrong to kill a human being simply to make life easier for society as a whole. If unborn children are human beings, which I have demonstrated through science and philosophy is the case, then we should not kill them to improve life for born people.

13. If pro-life people don't want abortions to happen, then why don't they promote using contraceptives in order to prevent unintended pregnancies?

The goal of the pro-life movement is to restore the right to life of unborn human beings. Does promoting contraception help or hinder that goal? I think it's safe to say contraception doesn't help that goal. Birth control pills and condoms don't teach people that unborn children are biological human beings who are entitled to the same basic rights you and I possess. To many people, contraception just prevents pregnancy, or it prevents a "potential person" (who will one day become a baby) from being created inside of a woman. There's nothing hypocritical about pro-life advocates not promoting contraception, because contraception doesn't do anything to reach our ultimate goal of changing public opinion and public policy to protect unborn children from harm. Promoting contraception may even detract from the goal of ending legal abortion.

In *Planned Parenthood v. Casey,* the Supreme Court said that *Roe v. Wade* "could not be repudiated without serious inequity to people who, for two decades of economic and social developments, have organized intimate relationships and made choices that define their views of themselves and their places in society, in reliance on the availability of abortion in the event that contraception should fail."[31] I'm all in favor of teaching people how to responsibly plan their families, but if contraception fosters the attitude that the interests of unborn children do not need to be taken into account when adults have sex, then contraception is a hindrance and not a help to the pro-life movement. If a child is conceived in spite of a couple's desire to stop him from coming into existence, then it is much more likely that child will be aborted to compensate for the failure of contraceptives. Pope St. John Paul II said in regards to this problem:

> It may be that many people use contraception with a view to excluding the subsequent temptation of abortion. But the negative values inherent in the "contraceptive mentality"—which is very different from responsible parenthood, lived in respect for the full truth of the conjugal act—are such that they in fact *strengthen this temptation when an unwanted life is conceived* [emphasis added]. Indeed, the pro-abortion culture is especially strong precisely where the Church's teaching on contraception is rejected.[32]

Promoting contraception may also reinforce attitudes toward sex and pregnancy that conflict with the goal of creating a culture of life. On one university campus, a group of students chastised me for not passing out condoms. I told them I didn't have to, because the campus health center gave away condoms for free. One man responded, "But the center is all the way on the other side of campus. I don't want to have to walk all the way over there just for condoms. You guys should be passing them out here." If this man was too lazy to walk a few hundred yards for condoms, why in the world would we expect him to work hard to provide for a child should the condom fail and his partner become pregnant?

Pro-life advocates should not be suckered into thinking that abortion is a public health problem that we have to alleviate by dispensing contraceptives as the cure. We must continue to teach our culture that abortion is a moral problem and that the unborn deserve cultural recognition and legal protection as a remedy to this problem. Granted, it will be easier to pass laws against abortion when fewer people seek abortion services, so there is value in developing strategies to reduce unintended pregnancies. But pro-life advocates should not have to compromise their belief that the unborn are human beings so that everyone can play nice together. Instead, we must refocus on finding better ways to achieve the goal of restoring legal protection for unborn human beings and not become caught up in simply reducing the need for abortion.

14. I can't stand hypocritical anti-abortion people. How many children have they adopted? Will they pay for all these children they don't want aborted? Most of them are men who shouldn't even be talking about the issue in the first place!

An *ad hominem* fallacy occurs when a person tries to refute his opponent not by attacking his argument but by attacking the opponent himself. Questions addressed to pro-life advocates such as "How many children have you adopted?" or "Do you also oppose the death penalty along with abortion?" are really just veiled attacks that try to paint the pro-life advocate as inconsistent or a bad person.

The reason the *ad hominem* tactic is a fallacy is because the strength of an argument has nothing to do with the character of the person making the argument. Sweet, kind people can be wrong. Mean, vicious people can be right. To demonstrate this, the pro-life advocate may admit, for the sake of argument, that he is as bad as the critic says he is (even if that is not true). The pro-life advocate can even facetiously claim to be *worse* than what the pro-choice critic accuses him of being. After admitting to being an awful person, he should simply ask how his character defects affect the injustice of killing the unborn through abortion. The conversation might go like this:

Pro-choicer: How many children have you adopted?

Pro-lifer: How does that relate to whether abortion should be legal?

Pro-choicer: You say abortion should be illegal and people should adopt unwanted children, but if you haven't adopted any children, then you're a hypocrite.

Pro-lifer: Let's say you're right—I'm a hypocrite who will never adopt children. Let's say further that I hate children and I'm just an all-around bad guy. How do any of my character defects justify keeping it legal to kill children through abortion?

Pro-choicer: They're not children, they're fetuses! [Now we're back to the one question that matters most: "What are the unborn?"]

Another way to respond to allegations of inconsistency is to *turn the tables* on the pro-choice accuser. Take the case of a pro-choice advocate who actively opposes war and the death penalty because she believes these things violate human rights. She might criticize the pro-life advocate who does not share her views:

Pro-choicer: So you say you're pro-life, but are you opposed to the death penalty?

Pro-lifer: What if I supported the death penalty? How does that relate to whether abortion should be legal or not?

Pro-choicer: Because if you support the death penalty, then you're not truly pro-life.

Pro-lifer: Do you support the death penalty?

Pro-choicer: I'm against it.

Pro-lifer: Why?

Pro-choicer: Because every year innocent people are wrongfully executed for crimes they didn't commit.

Pro-lifer: But isn't it inconsistent for you to oppose the killing of innocent people through capital punishment and not also oppose the killing of innocent people through abortion? More human beings will die from abortion by lunchtime today than have been killed by the death penalty since it was reinstated by the Supreme Court in 1976. Doesn't that concern you?

Pro-choicer: But that's different. I'm talking about born people. [Once again, we're back to the one question that matters most.]

This approach also exposes the illogic of pro-choice advocates' claiming men may not oppose abortion because they will never be pregnant. Many pro-choice advocates also oppose things that will never affect them. For example, they might oppose child abuse even though they themselves will never be an abused child. Furthermore, pro-choice advocates are inconsistent if they try to silence male pro-life advocates who cannot become pregnant but don't try to silence pro-choice men or post-menopausal pro-choice women, both of whom cannot become pregnant. In fact, the *Roe v. Wade* decision was handed down by seven men, so if men should not be allowed to have an opinion on abortion, then *Roe v. Wade* should be overturned.

The lesson to be learned here is that both pro-life and pro-choice people should refrain from attacking each other personally and instead discuss the status of unborn children and whether we have the right to kill those children because they are unwanted.

15. Does the Bible teach that abortion is wrong?

The Bible nowhere explicitly discusses the morality of abortion. This is not surprising, because in the ancient world the preferred method of ending the life of a small child was not abortion but simply leaving him exposed to the elements shortly after birth.

But because the Bible does not explicitly condemn abortion does not mean it condones it. There are many things the Bible does not condemn (such as airplane hijackings) that we can be sure are not condoned by the biblical authors. When it comes to abortion, we know that God forbids the killing of human beings (Exod. 20:13; Prov. 6:16-17), because human beings are made in the image of God (Genesis 1:26-27; 9:6). Since science and philosophy inform us that the unborn are human beings, it follows that abortion is wrong. John Paul II wrote in *The Gospel of Life*:

The texts of Sacred Scripture never address the question of deliberate abortion and so do not directly and specifically condemn it. But they show such great respect for the human being in the mother's womb that they require as a logical consequence that God's commandment "You shall not kill" be extended to the unborn child as well.[33]

Some pro-choice advocates argue that some parts of the Bible imply that a human being becomes a person after birth, and therefore abortion is not wrong. One example is Genesis 2:7: "[T]hen the Lord God formed the man out of the dust of the ground and blew into his nostrils the breath of life, and the man became a living being." Pro-choice advocates say that since Adam became "a living being" when God breathed "the breath of life" into him, until a baby breathes outside of the womb, he is not a person.

If this argument were valid, it would justify infanticide as well as abortion, since many babies do not breathe for up to a minute after birth. Secondly, the unborn do breathe before birth, but instead of breathing through their mouths, they breathe through an umbilical cord. Before they develop the umbilical cord, unborn children absorb oxygen through the lining of their cells in a process called respiration. I don't think the pro-choice advocate would say that a baby has to breathe through his mouth in order to be considered human, because there are some injured born humans who must breathe through a tube in their throat.

Finally, God had to infuse a human soul directly into Adam (or breathe the "breath of life" into him), since Adam was the first human being. All other human beings come into existence from other living human beings, so the requirement that God must "breathe" life into them as he did to Adam is unsupportable.

The other favorite passage of religious pro-choice advocates is Exodus 21:22-24, which describes what the punishment should be for accidentally harming an unborn child. The text reads, "When men strive together, and hurt a woman with child, so that there is a miscarriage, and yet no harm follows, the one who hurt her shall be fined, according as the woman's husband shall lay upon him; and he shall pay as the judges determine. If any harm follows, then you shall give life for life, eye for eye, tooth for tooth, hand for hand, foot for foot."

Critics use this passage to argue that if the unborn were fully persons, then the punishment for killing them would be not a fine but the death penalty. Therefore, the fetus isn't a person.

How does it follow that because someone is fined for *accidentally* killing an unborn child, God would judge lightly the *intentional* killing of an unborn child through abortion? After all, there is a punishment, so the child has some value and is not equivalent to disposable medical waste. In the preceding verses a man who accidentally kills his slave is not punished, but in the next verse intentionally killing a slave is grounds for serious punishment, possibly even the death penalty.[34] We simply have no other biblical directive about how to punish someone if he intentionally kills an unborn child, which is what happens in modern abortions. Therefore, it is inaccurate to say the Bible allows intentional abortion just because it advocates a lighter punishment for accidentally causing a miscarriage.

16. Does the Catholic Church teach that abortion is wrong?

Paragraphs 2270 and 2271 of the *Catechism of the Catholic Church* state, "Human life must be respected and protected absolutely from the moment of conception. From the first moment of his existence, a human being must be recognized as having the rights of a person—among which is the inviolable right of every innocent being to life. . . . Direct abortion, that is to say, abortion willed either as an end or a means, is gravely contrary to the moral law."

This teaching of the Catholic Church is not new, and in fact Christians have condemned abortion since the earliest apostolic times. A first-century Christian document called the *Didache* states, "You shall not use potions. You shall not procure abortion, nor destroy a newborn child."[35] By A.D. 314 the ecclesial Council of Ancyra thought it was being "lenient" in reducing a woman's penance for procuring an abortion to ten years of fasting.[36]

Some pro-choice advocates claim that the Church has not defined when life begins, and since theologians such as Augustine speculated that it began anywhere from forty to eighty days after conception, abortion is not wrong. But those Church Fathers who believed ensoulment occurred after conception never endorsed the view that abortion was moral. Second, they operated under the mistaken view of human development espoused by the philosopher Aristotle. He thought that unborn children progressed through vegetable and animal stages of life before their bodies were "animated" with a rational soul and they became human beings later in pregnancy. Other early Church writers such as Tertullian made it clear that it does not matter "whether you take away a life that is born, or destroy one that is coming to birth. That is a man which is going to be one; you have the fruit already in its seed" (*Apology* 9:8 [A.D. 197]). Tertullian himself believed "the soul also begins from conception; life taking its commencement at the same moment and place that the soul does" (*The Soul* 27).

Early Christians did agree that it was a grave evil to kill the developing human life in the womb, regardless of whether or not God had "formed" it with a soul.

This is articulated by St. Basil the Great, who said in the fourth century, "The woman who purposely destroys her unborn child is guilty of murder. With us there is no nice enquiry as to its being formed or unformed."[37]

The Church Fathers did not know as much about human development as we do today. If they knew about modern genetics, then they would wholeheartedly affirm that the unborn are human beings made in the image of God. Moral theologian William May concludes,

> St. Thomas, were he alive today and cognizant of the biological evidence known today, would not hesitate in concluding that the *body* that comes to be when fertilization is completed is indubitably a *human* body and hence that its organizing and vivifying principle can only be a *human soul*, an intellectual or spiritual soul.[38]

The teaching magisterium of the Catholic Church upholds the universally held tradition that abortion is a grave evil. Pope John Paul II issued an authoritative statement on the subject in his encyclical *The Gospel of Life*:

> Given such unanimity in the doctrinal and disciplinary tradition of the Church, Paul VI was able to declare that this tradition is unchanged and

unchangeable. Therefore, by the authority which Christ conferred upon Peter and his Successors, in communion with the Bishops—who on various occasions have condemned abortion and who in the aforementioned consultation, albeit dispersed throughout the world, have shown unanimous agreement concerning this doctrine—*I declare that direct abortion, that is, abortion willed as an end or as a means, always constitutes a grave moral disorder*, since it is the deliberate killing of an innocent human being. This doctrine is based upon the natural law and upon the written Word of God, is transmitted by the Church's Tradition and taught by the ordinary and universal Magisterium.[39]

17. Abortion is certainly an important issue, but it's not the only issue. Shouldn't pro-lifers broaden their focus and work to end other threats to human life, such as the death penalty, war, poverty, sex trafficking, and racism?

Abortion is not the only issue today any more than slavery was the only issue facing America in the 1860s. However, a strong case can be made that abortion is the most *important* issue facing America today, because it involves the loss of our most fundamental right (the right to life), and it affects millions of human beings. But even though abortion occurs on such a large scale, should pro-life advocates focus solely on abortion and neglect other issues?

Cardinal Joseph Bernardin once said that life issues such as abortion, euthanasia, the death penalty, and unjust war were like a "seamless garment" that should not be torn apart. In a speech given at Fordham University in 1983, Cardinal Bernardin said, "If one contends, as we do, that the right of every fetus to be born should be protected by civil law and supported by civil consensus, then our moral, political and economic responsibilities do not stop at the moment of birth."[40]

Some people seize on Bernardin's praiseworthy call to consistency and say that the pro-life movement should be for all life and not just unborn life. But the position of "being for all life" is vague and confusing. Does that mean pro-life advocates have to oppose antibiotics because they kill bacterial "life"? Even if these critics argued that we should be "for all human life," what would that mean? Does that mean pro-life advocates have to solve *every* problem that affects human beings from conception to natural death? Do pro-life advocates have to work to solve hunger, war, disease, human trafficking, poverty, discrimination, illiteracy, and slow Internet connections?

The goal of the pro-life movement is to secure the *right to life* of all human beings from conception to natural death. That means it should be illegal to kill an innocent human being intentionally, regardless of that human being's level of function or location. The pro-life movement's job is also not to secure the best possible life for all human beings because such a goal is impossible for one movement. All movements that care about doing good limit the scope of their activities because if they tried to do everything, they would accomplish nothing.

Even the pro-choice movement doesn't try to protect all "choices." Many pro-choice advocates oppose the choice not to work in a labor union, the choice to own a firearm, or the choice not to hire a person because of his sexual behavior. Just as pro-choice advocates can restrict their definition of *choice* to mean "access to legal contraception and abortion," pro-life advocates should restrict their focus to "the legally recognized right to life of all human beings."

The Catholic Church has held that under some circumstances the death penalty can be a moral choice, and just war can be used as a weapon of last resort.[41] These acts are evil in circumstance or degree, unlike abortion, which is evil in every circumstance due to the nature of the act itself. The seamless-garment approach also doesn't mean that pro-life advocates must confront these other "life" issues with the same energy or resources. Cardinal Bernardin himself clarified this point in a later address: "It is not necessary or possible for every person to engage in each issue, but it is both possible and necessary for the Church as a whole to cultivate a conscious explicit connection among the several issues."[42]

18. My friend is pregnant and thinking of getting an abortion. What should I do?

While you may have a good relationship with your friend, you probably lack the professional training needed to help someone manage an unintended pregnancy. That is why the best thing you can do is to take your friend to a pregnancy resource center.

Some pregnancy resource centers offer discounted prenatal care, ultrasound, housing, job placement, low-cost or free baby supplies, adoption referrals, and myriad other helpful services. They can be found online or by referral through your local parish. Learn about these centers and make a commitment to personally take your friend to one (don't just give her a phone number).

Ultimately, you must show your friend that she is *already* a mother, even if she claims she is not ready to *become* a mother. She needs to see that choosing abortion will involve choosing to be the mother of a dead baby instead of being the mother of a living baby. She must also see that you are truly her friend, and it is out of the love you have for her that you want to help her avoid the trauma of abortion.

How should you talk to someone who is considering abortion? First, let her know you feel sorry that she has to contemplate this choice and that you are there so she doesn't have to be alone when making her decision. Reassure her that she has a full range of options and that no situation is hopeless. Refrain from commenting on how she could have avoided the situation (such as refraining from sex) because that won't help her feeling of hopelessness.

You have the power to open up options to her she never knew existed, but those options will be helpful only if you listen to her and understand her specific situation. For example, can she get help from parents, partner, friends? What is her life situation? How does she feel about adoption? It is imperative that you act as a "safe place" where your friend can seek help and not be someone who will chastise her. You may address your friend's spiritual and moral choices after her baby is safe. Until then, building a trusting relationship with her is the only way to safeguard both her well-being and the baby's life.

If your friend seems undeterred, you might consider using graphic pictures of abortion in order to change her mind. Greg Cunningham of the Center for Bio-Ethical Reform (CBR) puts it succinctly: "If a woman isn't more terrified of abortion than pregnancy, then her child will die." CBR successfully uses graphic pictures to show people the truth about abortion. I have seen graphic pictures cause women to walk out of abortion mills and other women to cancel appointments at these mills. However, these pictures should be used with the utmost care, and you should always warn people to whom you plan to show graphic images. Hopefully this approach will help your friend see what abortion really is and, as a result, not want any part in it.

Finally, never assume the baby is safe, even if your friend has visited a pregnancy resource center. Email or call to make sure that your friend has not run into problems or is about to succumb to the temptation of abortion. Many women in the early stages of pregnancy, when the only sign of the unborn child's existence is nausea, can be easily swayed to trade this hardship to have their "normal" lives and futures back. Only intervention and the promise of help can overcome this tremendous temptation.

19. I know someone who has had an abortion. How can I reach out to her and help her overcome her pain and guilt?

Post-abortion grief is the result of a mother's coming to grips with the reality of abortion. In such cases, women suffer arguably the worst feeling a human being can endure: the feeling of failing to protect someone who was literally a part of them. Even worse, these women understand that they were involved in killing their children.

While their circumstances may differ, each of these women also suffer from society's failure to provide an adequate grieving system for abortion stress. For example, a mother who miscarries is validated as having lost a child and is allowed to grieve appropriately over that loss. A woman who has had an abortion, however, is told that it was "the best decision she could have made," it was "her choice," or it was "not a big deal, just a medical procedure." After all, anyone can see the awkwardness of grieving over the death of a child when the death was planned and paid for by one or both of the child's parents. However, ignoring the problem is also a poor solution for the pain these women (and men) experience.

Some women feel the grief of an abortion immediately following the procedure, while others don't feel the onset of symptoms for many years. Emotional distress is most likely to occur around the anniversary of either the abortion or the expected due date of the baby. A post-abortive woman may also feel an onset of regret about her abortion in the presence of pregnant women, during discussions about abortion, or when she is in the presence of families with small children, especially children who are the same age as her aborted child would have been.

The most important skill to have when talking to a woman who has had an abortion is the skill of *listening*. A common temptation (usually faced by men) is to try to say something that will make the woman feel better or solve her problem. However, just as abortion doesn't change the fact that a woman was pregnant, post-abortion counseling does not take away the fact that an abortion happened and that a child has died.

Listen to how the woman is feeling, and ask questions to show you care and are interested in her well-being. "How long have you had these feelings?" "How are you handling everything since the abortion?" You can't take away her pain, but you can take away her loneliness by being there for her.

Do not try to steer the conversation in the direction you think it should go. If she wants to speak of a four-week-old embryo as a "baby," let her. If she needs to cry, yell, or not talk at all, let her. Above all, keep her and her healing as the center of your focus. The grieving process is different for everyone. The woman should be given whatever time she needs to work through it.

Avoid your own commentary on abortion and avoid trying to minimize her pain by noting the gestational age of her child, her life situation, or her reasons for having the abortion. Let her know you feel sorry for her pain, but do not tell her that you know how she feels. If you haven't had an abortion, you do not know how she feels. Even if you have had an abortion, you can't know how *she* feels as a unique individual. If you treat her grief as being the equivalent of grief over the death of a born child, you will probably act with the appropriate amount of compassion.

Finally, while you may be able to help your friend start to confront her (or his) past guilt and pain related to the abortion experience, you should refer your friend to a trained counselor to help her find long-lasting healing. Without betraying your friend's confidence, ask your local priest or pregnancy resource center if they know of any post-abortion healing ministries. You may also want to contact national ministries such as Rachel's Vineyard that offer weekend retreats for those who are looking to cope with post-abortion grief.[43]

20. What can I do to end abortion?

Martin Luther King Jr. wrote in his "Letter from a Birmingham Jail," "[F]reedom is never voluntarily given by the oppressor; it must be demanded by the oppressed." Unfortunately, unborn children are incapable of demanding their own right to life, and so other people must argue on their behalf. The best thing you can do to end abortion is to be an articulate defender of the pro-life view. You can be someone who is not afraid to speak up for the unborn in a gracious and persuasive way. By explicitly talking about abortion and framing it as an issue involving human rights and equal treatment, pro-life advocates can recapture the public's imagination and rally it to the defense of the innocent.

Pro-life advocates must not be afraid to talk about abortion, because pro-choice advocates have done everything they can not to bring up abortion in public. They refer to abortion as "reproductive health care" and focus almost exclusively on access to contraception. After researching pro-life organizations who engage in dialogue on public university campuses, Professor Jon A. Shields of the University of Virginia concluded that pro-choice advocates seem either unwilling or unprepared to confront the growing philosophical sophistication of pro-life advocates. He describes how pro-life groups have to "beg" pro-choice groups to debate them and how national pro-choice organizations instruct their university affiliates not to "waste time talking to anti-choice people."[44] Frances Kissling, the cofounder of Catholics for Choice, and Kate Michelman, cofounder of NARAL Pro-Choice America (which used to call itself the National Abortion Rights Action League until in 2003 it stopped spelling out its acronym), co-authored an article admitting that Shields is right:

> Twenty years ago, being pro-life was déclassé. Now it is a respectable point of view. How did this happen? In the 1970s, the arguments were simple and polarized: Abortion was either murder or a woman's right to control her body. Now, we rarely hear them [pro-lifers] talk about murdering babies. Instead, they present a sophisticated philosophical and political challenge. Caring societies, they say,

seek to expand inclusion into "the human community." Those once excluded, such as women and minorities, are now equal. Why not welcome the fetus (who, after all, is us) into our community?[45]

Pro-life advocates should have confidence that their arguments are sound and persuasive and that we must continue the hard work of communicating them to society as a whole. But along with personally engaging those who disagree, pro-life advocates should ask themselves how they can use their individual gifts to help the unborn in other ways. Consider how you would answer the following questions.

Do I have time to give to the pro-life movement by:
- Volunteering at a local pregnancy center?
- Going to the sidewalk of an abortion clinic for one hour a week to pray or counsel women who are going in to obtain abortions?
- Making phone calls or passing out literature in support of pro-life legislation?

Do I have talents to serve the pro-life movement by:
- Creating art or social media for pro-life organizations?
- Learning how to speak on abortion and give pro-life presentations to schools and churches in my community?
- Spreading the pro-life message through performance

art (song, film, dance, acting, photography, etc.)?

Do I have treasure to help the pro-life movement by:
- Donating a percentage of my monthly salary to an organization working to secure the right to life of all human beings?
- Donating the services of my business to help a pro-life group?
- Supplying or donating baby products that are in good condition to local pregnancy centers?

One of the best ways you can end abortion is by living a life of chastity and refraining from sexual activity until marriage. By doing this, any child you help create will come into existence in an act of love between two people who have promised not only to be faithful to one another but to be open to God's blessing them with children made in his image and likeness.

Finally, don't despair, even when the cause of standing up for the unborn can be frustrating. Standing up for truth in a world that wants only to hear what is pleasant is tough. Even if you are gracious in defending the unborn, it is likely that critics will say you are anti-woman, a religious fanatic, or a bigot who is imposing your morality on others. But this can't stop us from doing what is right and loving our neighbor—regardless of how young our neighbor is.

About the Author

Trent Horn is an apologist and speaker for Catholic Answers. He specializes in pro-life issues as well as outreach to atheists and agnostics. He holds a master's degree in theology from Franciscan University of Steubenville.

Endnotes

1   Lydia Saad, "Pro-Choice Americans at Record-Low 41%," Gallup poll, May 23, 2012, http://www.gallup.com/poll/154838/pro-choice-americans-record-low.aspx.

2   Hart Research, June 2012 Poll for National Women's Law Center and Planned Parenthood Federation of America.

3   NBC News/*Wall Street Journal* Survey, HART/McINTURFF Study #13018, January 12-15, 2013, http://msnbcmedia.msn.com/i/MSNBC/Sections/A_Politics/_Today_Stories_Teases/Supreme-court-question.pdf.

4   Pew Research Center, "Young Adults Least Likely Age Group to Know Roe v. Wade about Abortion," January 22, 2013, http://www.pewresearch.org/daily-number/young-adults-least-likely-age-group-to-know-roe-v-wade-about-abortion/.

5   Lawrence B. Finer et. al., "Reasons U.S. Women Have Abortions: Quantitative and Qualitative Perspectives," *Perspectives on Sexual and Reproductive Health* 37, no. 3 (2005):110–118.

6   Gonzales v. Carhart, 550 U.S. 124 (2007), section I-A.

7   R.K. Jones, L.B. Finer, S. and Singh, *Characteristics of U.S. Abortion Patients 2008* (New York: Guttmacher Institute, 2010).

8   Pope John Paul II, *Evangelium Vitae* 99.

9   Blackmun wrote, "We need not resolve the difficult question of when life begins. When those trained in the respective disciplines of medicine, philosophy, and theology are unable to arrive at any consensus, the judiciary, at this point in the development of man's knowledge, is not in a position to speculate as to the answer": Roe v. Wade, 410 U.S. 113 (1973), sec. 9, par. B.

10 In 2011, 12,664 people were murdered in the United States, with 8,583 of the murders occurring with a firearm. See http://www.fbi.gov/about-us/cjis/ucr/crime-in-the-u.s/2011/crime-in-the-u.s.-2011/tables/expanded-homicide-data-table-8.

11 Doe v. Bolton, 410 U.S. 179, sec. 4, par. C: "We agree with the District Court, 319 F.Supp. at 1058, that the medical judgment may be exercised in the light of all factors—physical, emotional, psychological, familial, and the woman's age—relevant to the well-being of the patient. All these factors may relate to health. This allows the attending physician the room he needs to make his best medical judgment."

12 Warren Hern, "Is Pregnancy Really Normal?" *Family Planning Perspectives* 3, no. 1 (January 1971).

13 See Norma McCorvey, *Won by Love* (Nashville: Thomas Nelson Publishers, 1997).

14 Leading embryologist Keith L. Moore states, "The blood is circulating and the heart begins to beat on the 21st or the 22nd day": Keith L. Moore and T.V.N. Persaud, *The Developing Human: Clinically Oriented Embryology*, 9th ed. (Philadelphia: Saunders, 2011), 64.

15 E.L. Potter, M.D., and J.M. Craig, M.D., *Pathology of the Fetus and the Infant*, 3rd ed. (Chicago: Year Book Medical Publishers, 1975), vii.

16 Ronan O'Rahilly and Fabiola Müller, *Human Embryology and Teratology*, 2nd ed. (New York: Wiley-Liss, 1996), 8. Among embryologists, the preferred term for the beginning of life is *fertilization*, especially since, as I discussed earlier, *fertilization* and *conception* sometimes have different meanings.

17 David Boonin, *A Defense of Abortion* (Cambridge: Cambridge University Press, 2003), 20.

18 Furthermore, an infant born into a reversible coma would be in the position of never having felt anything at all and thus would not be a person under this view.

19 As examples of this refusal, Blackmun lists Jacobson v. Massachusetts, 197 U.S. 11 (1905) (vaccination) and Buck v. Bell, 274 U.S. 200 (1927) (sterilization): Roe v. Wade, 410 U.S. 113 sec. 8.

20 See also Stephanie Gray, "A Kidney versus the Uterus," *Ethics & Medics* 34, no. 10 (October 2009).

21 See Kennedy v. Louisiana, 554 U.S. 407 (2008).

22 Note that everything I've said about rape also applies to the horror associated with pregnancies that result from incest, such as when a father rapes his own daughter. Saying that the child who is created is a genetic monster who shouldn't be allowed to live is offensive to the people who were conceived in incest and have the same appearance as anyone else.

23 Barbara J. Syska; Thomas W. Hilgers, M.D.; and Dennis O'Hare, "An Objective Model for Estimating Criminal Abortions and Its Implications for Public Policy" in Thomas Hilgers, M.D.; Dennis J. Horan; and David Mall, eds., *New Perspectives on Human Abortion* (Frederick, Maryland: University Publications of America, 1981), 171.

24 Laurie D. Elam-Evans, Lilo T. Strauss, et al., "Abortion Surveillance, United States—2000," Table 19 (Centers for Disease Control), http://www.cdc.gov/mmwr/preview/mmwrhtml/ss5212a1.htm#tab19.

25 Mary Steichen Calderone, "Illegal Abortion as a Public Health

Problem," *American Journal of Public Health Nations Health* 50, no. 7 (July 1960): 949.

26 "Maternal Mortality Rates," *The World Fact Book* (Washington, D.C.: Central Intelligence Agency, 2010), https://cia.gov/library/publications/the-world-factbook/rankorder/2223rank.html.

27 In Great Britain infanticide is recognized as a separate crime as a result of the Infanticide Act of 1938, while in places like the United States there is no separate charge, but the distinction is present in the severity of the sentence.

28 Warren Hern, *Abortion Practice* (Philadelphia: J.B. Lippincott Company, 1984), 106.

29 Thomas Murphy Goodwin, "Medicalizing Abortion Decisions," *First Things* (March 1996), http://www.firstthings.com/index.php?permalink=article&entry_permalink=2007/10/003-medicalizing-abortion-decisions.

30 This approach to humanizing the unborn and refocusing the abortion issue comes from Scott Klusendorf, *The Case for Life* (Wheaton, Illinois: Crossway Books, 2009), 22-27.

31 Planned Parenthood of Southeastern Pa. v. Casey, (91-744), 505 U.S. 833 (1992).

32 *Evangelium Vitae* 13.

33 *Evangelium Vitae* 61.

34 Exod. 21:20-21.

35 *Didache* 2:1–2.

36 Council of Ancyra, canon 21.

37 St. Basil the Great, *First Canonical Letter*, canon 2.

38 William May, *Catholic Bioethics and the Gift of Life* (Huntington, Indiana: Our Sunday Visitor, 2000), 164-165.

39 *Evangelium Vitae* 62.

40 Joseph Cardinal Bernardin, "A Consistent Ethic of Life: An American-Catholic Dialogue," Gannon Lecture, Fordham University, December 6, 1983, http://hnp.org/publications/hnpfocus/BConsistentEthic1983.pdf.

41 For the Catholic view of the death penalty and just war, see paragraphs 2267 and 2309 of the *Catechism of the Catholic Church*.

42 Joseph Cardinal Bernardin, "A Consistent Ethic of Life: Continuing the Dialogue," The William Wade Lecture Series, St. Louis University, March 11, 1984.

43 To learn more about Rachel's Vineyard, visit www.rachelsvineyard.org.

44 Jon A. Shields, *The Democratic Virtues of the Christian Right* (Princeton, New Jersey: Princeton University Press, 2009), 80.

45 Frances Kissling and Kate Michelman, "Abortion's Battle of Messages," *Los Angeles Times*, January 22, 2008.

Become part of the team.
Help support Catholic Answers.

Catholic Answers is an apostolate dedicated to serving Christ by bringing the fullness of Catholic truth to the world. We help good Catholics become better Catholics, bring former Catholics "home," and lead non-Catholics into the fullness of the Faith.

Catholic Answers neither asks for nor receives financial support from any diocese. The majority of its annual income is in the form of donations from individual supporters like you.

To make a donation by phone using your credit card, please speak with one of our customer service representatives at 888-291-8000.

To make a donation by check, please send a check payable to "Catholic Answers" to:

> Catholic Answers
> 2020 Gillespie Way
> El Cajon, CA 92020

To make a donation online, visit **catholic.com**.

catholic.com